ZANY ZOO

MAX KNIGHT
ZANY ZOO

**Cover and Full-Page Illustrations:
Matthew Simpson
Cartoon Vignettes: Don Ware**

BERKELEY

ISBN: 0-916147-40-1

Printed by Regent Press
Oakland, California
Manufactured in the United States of America

The Western town of Petaluma
has no connection with a puma.
The puma is a mountain lion
and has no Petaluma tie-on
but if you are a versifier
you try by hook or crook to tie her.
So, have a little sense of huma
and let me have this pome with puma.

CONTENTS

BIPEDS

The Emu

The emu is a nasty bird
of whom some people never heard.
He dwells in puzzles and Australia
and is a sordid sort, I tellya:
He never flies and never sings,
and when he bites your hand, it stings.
Don't emulate the emu, man,
and just avoid him if you can.
  You do not like the emu?
  I don't blemu.

The Ostrich

The ostrich is an optimist.
Unwelcome notions are dismissed,
and quite forgotten are the threats
posed long ago by ladies' hats.
The ostrich says: "The world is grand."
(And where it ain't, there's always sand.)

The Flamingo

Flamingos have long pretzel necks,
which they can amorously flex.
I wonder: If two flams embrace,
would not their necks then interlace
and, if their necking gets too hot,
tie in a strangulating knot?

('twould kill any flamingo,
1, 2, 3, bingo!)

Doves

What lovely symbol is the charming dove!
It stands for peace and for romantic love.
When doves walk on the ground,
                  you like to feed them,
but when they're in the air
                  you do not need them
for on the ground you watch them
                  with affection
but when they're overhead
                  you need protection.
I like them best when they are shown
                  (with hearts)
on wedding notices or friendship cards.

The Albatross

Isn't the albatross terrific?
Proud glides he over the Pacific
with wings spread wide ten feet or more
as high above the waves they soar.
  To watch him in majestic flight
is surely an inspiring sight
and triggers a poetic itch —
you need not be a Coleridge.
  I like the albatross a lot
(around the neck though, I'd say not).

Endangered Species

The Condor

The condor is extremely rare.
Its head is bald, its neck is bare —
  it is no special beauty
  (but beauty is no duty);
  its diet choice lacks culture
  (but, then, it is a vulture).
Since near extinction is its breed,
forget its looks, forget its feed,
  and whether you are really fond or
  not fond of vultures:
                    Save the Condor!

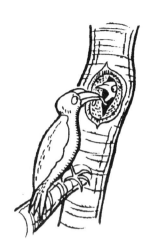

The Hornbill

The hornbill feeds his family
that's trapped inside a hollow tree.
He plasters carefully the cleft
till just a tiny slit is left
and hunts for insects far and wide.
She, with the young ones, stays inside,
trades freedom for security
until the chicks' maturity.
　She trusts that he will break the lock,
when time has come to free the flock.
　How rarely does one see a house
　with that much trust
　　　　　　　　from spouse to spouse.

Matthew D. Simpson

The Archeopteryx

In eras long ago,
              above the horsetail sticks,
soared high, majestically,
              the archeopteryx.*
He was a classic,
who lived in the Jurassic.
Once a Neanderthaler asked him: "Archy,
what do you eat? Fats, proteins,
              something starchy?"
The archeopteryx just shrugged:
              "Don't be absurd.
My diet? Worms, of course.
              I am an early bird."

---

*Primitive ancestor of birds, which lived in the the Jurassic
limestone of Bavaria, 200 million years ago.

The Stork

The stork enjoys mixed popularity
because he delivers posterity.

The Cuckoos

The cuckoos lay their eggs in nests
of other birds, as unbid guests.
Zoologists are much confused,
some are disgusted, some enthused:
they do not know how to appraise
the cuckoos' unconventional ways —
damn them as aberration
or hail as conservation?

The Arctic Tern

Of all the birds that fly or nest
the Arctic tern's the championest
by flying from the Arctic ice
to the Antarctic yearly twice.
To reach their annual breeding goal
a pair flies almost pole to pole.
When they arrive, the pair unpack,
then make a tern, and double back.

QUADRUPEDS

PEDESTRIANS
TREE CLIMBERS
WATER LOVERS

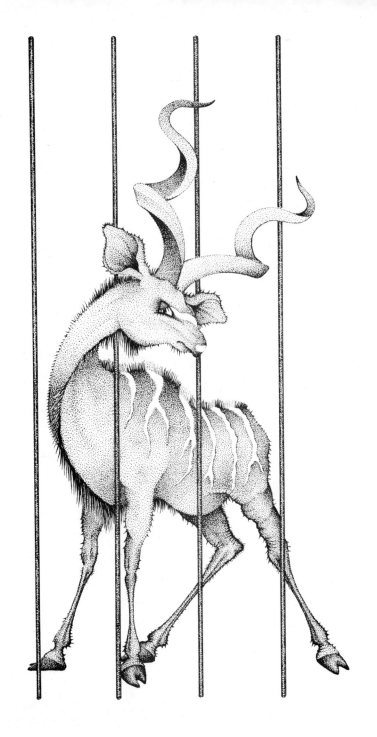

The Kudu

What can a kudu caged in a zoo do?
He's an antelope who cantelope
except by voodoo.
   If you were a kudu, what would you do?

The Camel

The camel, known as desert ship,
has a contemptuous upper lip.
Just watch him haughtily advance,
a picture of pure arrogance.
He thinks he is a genius,
much better than the rest of us,
and that we are creation's blight . . .
   Perhaps he's right.

Warthog Tragedy

A nubile warthog maiden,
she found no gent to embrace
because, although otherwise charming,
she had no warts on her face.

Matthew D. Simpson JAN.

The Wombat

The wombat dwelleth in his lair,
akin to the koala bear.
He's not a bat, he's not a wom,
but modest, cute, and frolicsome.
His tail is short, his legs quadruple,
his nose is bare, his pouch marsuple.
He is a truly friendly guy,
his ways are peaceful, meek, and shy.
  The wombat
  shuns combat.

The Buffalo

The Buffalo, the buffalo,
it does not know just where to go.
It once roamed happily the Plains
but white men hunted it from trains.
So when it faced annihilation,
men caged it in a reservation.
Confined here, though,
                its plight was great.—
it could not freely *circulate*.
  But finally, when in this pickle,
  it found its freedom in a nickel.*

---

*Still, even here its days are gone;
it is squeezed out by Jefferson.

The Armadillo

The armadillo
can roll himself into a pillow
by tucking his face
inside his carapace.
It is little known
that in the Amazon
the he-madillo oft begets,
as eager father, quadruplets,
  while the she-madillo
  regards a family
  of only two or three
  as a social peccadillo.

Matthew E. Saipan Feb 20, '92

The Hyena

No beast is meaner
than the hyena.
How he does carry on
when he smells carrion!
And when blood he quaffs—
he laughs.

Yaks

Three yaks in Tibet were walking
along the mountain road
and on their trek were squawking
about their heavy load.
   Three sherpas spurned the mumbling
when the yaks bemoaned their pack
and let them have their grumbling,
yakety yakety yak.

Matthew D. Simpson

The Aardvark

The aardvark is an oddish creature.
He sports huge ears as special feature,
he never touches any plants
and feeds on termites and on ants.
He digs them with his pig-like snout;
his foreclaws pack a hefty clout.
He picks up ants with sticky tongue.
His tail's unnaturally long.

I find the aardvark
aawkward.

The Elephant

When animals were gathering
to crown the mighty lion king,
the elephant alone objected
protesting: "He was not elected!
I don't owe any loyalty
to monarchy and royalty,
I am no prince's fawning fan,
because I'm a Republican."

Protodeer

In prehistoric caves is seen
the artwork of the Pleistocene.
The "deer" shown on those wall graffiti
look much like elk, moose, or wapiti,
but what the artists really inked
were deer forefathers, long extinct.
These ancestors were an elite
whose antlers spanned eleven feet.
It saves a headache in a way
that they are not around today
because those blessed with hunters' luck,
just for the horns would need a truck.

The Horse

If speech were given to the horse,
what it might say, I would endorse
because it's horse sense that we need,
whether from stallion or from steed.
Besides, it's known from North to South
that truth comes from the horse's mouth.

The Cat

You may own a shirt,
you may own a hat,
you may own a dog—
but you won't own a cat.

You may own a goldmine,
a castle or two,
a yacht, and great treasures —
but a Cat will own You.

Matthew T. Simpson '82

TREE CLIMBERS

The Sloth

The sloth, this furry, three-toed clown,
lives in the treetops upside down.
He knows the world is topsy-turvy —
what's black is white,

            what's straight is curvy,
the good are weak, the bad are strong,
what's left is right,

            what's right is wrong.
Men watch this turmoil with concern
and do not know which way to turn . . .
    The sloth solves this paralysis
    and sees the world just as it is.

The Chimpanzee

The chimpanzee, the chimpanzee
is said to be as wise as we.
But I suspect, but I suspect
there is some aspect we neglect,
and that is that the chimpanzee
does not build war machinery
but dwelleth peaceful in his tree
and lives his life, lets others be.
The chimpanzee, the chimpanzee
may be a wiser ape than we.

MATTHEW SIMPSON

The Bears

The black bear and the polar bear
would make a fascinating pair.
I don't believe they ever mate
but it is fun to speculate:
How would an offspring in their lair
turn out? As gray bear? zebra bear?

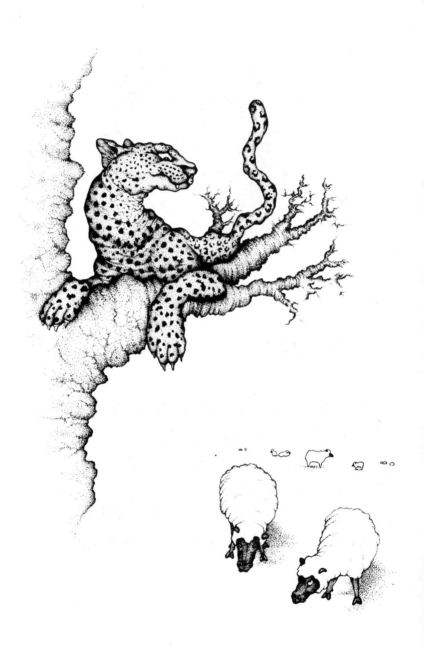

The Leopard

If you keep a flock of sheep,
you need a shepherd.
Not a leopard.
(He would jeopardize 'em,
then leopardize 'em.)

The Panda

The giant panda lives in China.
He is a very picky diner.
He eats no insects, grasses, roots,
but only dainty bamboo shoots.
In pairing he is also picky,
and finding him a mate is tricky.
In zoos throughout the world they need him
and try with eagerness to breed him,
but pandas locked up in a crate
don't usually cooperate.
   The pandas hide in Szech-yu-an,
where pandas sometimes catch you can.
   You think you'll catch a panda?
   I wanda.

Proboscis Monkey

The place where normally the nose is
takes for some monkeys the proboscis.
The tropic isle of Borneo
is where proboscis monkeys grow.
Their nose is longer than they need
and is a bother when they feed.
In zoos they scorn
the youngsters' tease,
turn up their nose at them,
    and sneeze.

The Beaver

The beaver has outlived men's passion
for beaver hats, when they were fashion.
He now lives relatively quiet
in rivers where he gets his diet.
He chops, however, with his teeth
relentlessly the toughest treeth.
He doesn't give a damn, you mean?
Not so! On dams he's very keen.
His teeth cut sharply like a cleaver
to build his home, as eager beaver.
    We chased him once for frippery,
and now begrudge the guy his tree.

Matthew D. Simpson Feb 18 '9

The Sea Otter

Eskimo women can relax
with babies carried on their backs,
whereas the cuddly otter Mummy
carries her babies on her tummy
while swimming on her back at sea,
a feat not copied easily.
    Sea otters are gourmets who eat
with gusto abalone meat,
and use a pebble when they crack
their shell tops with a gentle whack.
    To naughty otter kids Mom tells:
"Remember abalone shells!"

The Tuatara

On a remote New Zealand isle
a living fossil dwells in style.
The tuatara perseveres
for more than hundred million years,
an iguana-type of creature,
which has a very special feature:
It is, to everyone's surprise,
equipped by nature with three eyes.
Up, in mid-forehead, Number Three
sits well content and winks at thee —
   a puzzlement to scientists,
   a problem for optometrists.

Matthew D. Sniper '91

Hippolytus the Hippopotamus

The happy hippo Hippolyt
says hipps must diet to be fit.
   But then he waddles to the deli
and fills his belly.
   O Hippolyt, you hypocrit!

The Crocodile

In Africa, the crocodile
takes care of dental needs in style.
It opens wide its jaw to clean it
and let a bird pick and hygiene it.
It will not close its awesome gap
but curb its instinct and hold back.
   If someone picks on you, it could
(for all you know) be for your good.

The Platypus

An oddity is platypus,
a riddle fit for Oedipus.
It is a mammal,
like cow or camel,
but lays eggs like a chick.
   What a slick trick!

SIXPEDS

Matthew D. Snipson

The Ladybug

The polka-dotted ladybug –
does she have anyone to hug?
I trust she has a boybug chum,
where else would babybugs come from?

The Termites

The termites, on their mating day,
join thousands in a dance display.
Mating has always seemed to me
strictly an act of privacy.
  But termites
  are no hermites.

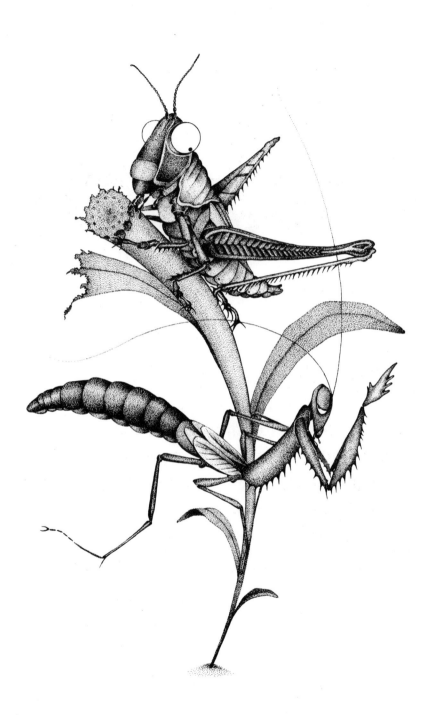

Grasshoppers

It makes you think, if you have focused
upon the mantis and the locust.
The hungry locust never stops
when it starts gobbling up our crops;
its appetite just never ends.
 You cannot say, though, it pretends,
 whereas the mantis eats its prey,
 then piously sits up to pray.

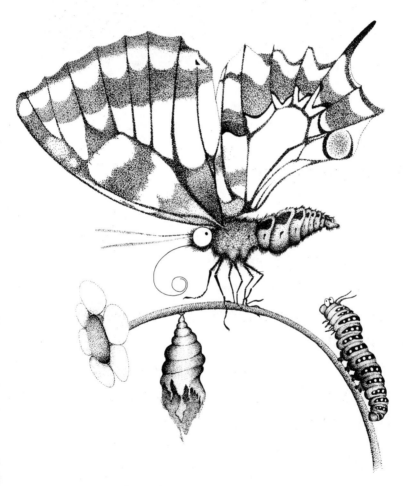

MATT SIMPSON

The Butterfly

The butterfly, if it survives,
is fortunate to have three lives.
At first, when it's a caterpillar,
it's prey to every bird as killer.
To flee its fate, it changes soon
conveniently to a cocoon.
This is much safer. But its lot
is now to hunker in one spot.
So finally it has its day
and sails as butterfly away.
    How lucky, if a human could
change bods, when one's no longer good,
by swallowing perhaps a dosis
of pills for such metamorphosis.
    Think deep, friend, when a butterfly
the next time you see flutter by.

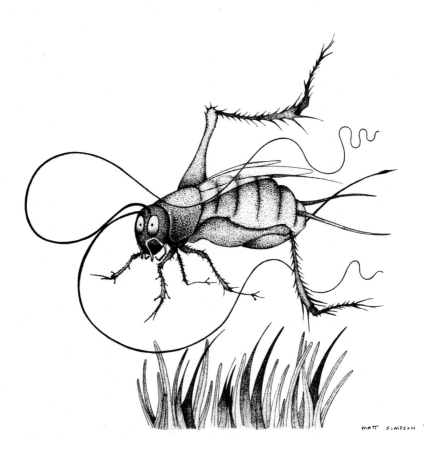

MATT SIMPSON '91

The Cricket

You hear but rarely see a cricket.
It chirps along in trees and thicket,
and with its pretty melody
delights us anonymously.
The poets and composers hail
the robin, lark, and nightingale,
but when the crickets sing their song,
no poet wags his silver tongue.
　I'm not surprised to see their picket,
　which reads: "No fair! It isn't cricket!"

The Gnats

The gnat is a peculiar thing —
a wisp of nothing with a sting.
Gnats like a picnic and the beach
and fly so close yet out of reach.
They suck the blood and prick the skin
of you, your friends, your next of kin.
You rarely catch them when they park,
and if you do, they leave a mark.
But even a successful slap
will come too late — they have your sap.
  You plan a picnic in a spot
  with gnats abuzz? You'd better gnot.

Matthew D. Simpson March 8 '92

Bee Work Ethics

What bees consider "women's place"
must be regarded a disgrace:
the female diligently works,
the lazy male sits back and smirks.

Male humans envy wistfully
the social system of the bee.

OCTOPEDS PLUS

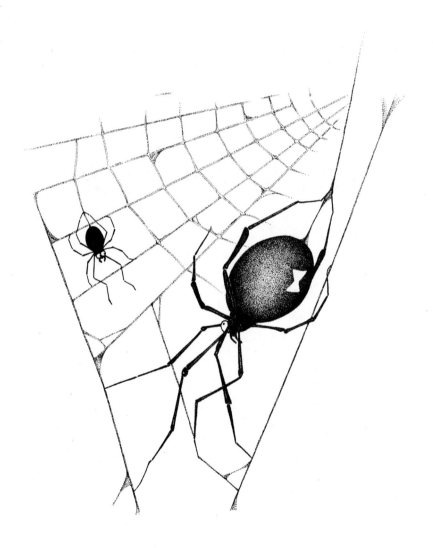

Matthew D. Swanson 91

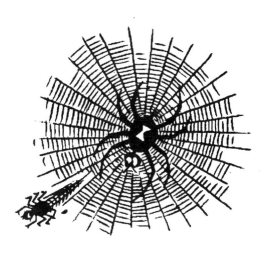

The Black Widow

Black widows flourish on a scale
that dwarfs the tiny spider male.
The wedding gives him such a scare,
he wraps her first with silver snare,
which buys him just enough delay
when love is done to run away.
But if he's not enough alert,
she snags and chomps him for dessert.
   I'll say the amorous black widow
   has something wrong with her libido.

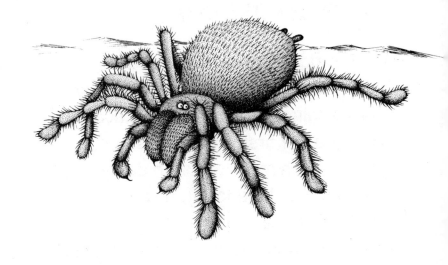

The Tarantula

The tarantula is hairy
and scary.
He comes out nights
and bites.
  Be wary!

Matthew D. Simpson '92 JAN 2

Octopus —
Wrong Number

The octopus, when floating in the sea,
saw tentacles as inconsistency.
They should be octacles, he said,
or he be tentopus instead.

Matthew W. Simpson Dec 1, '92

The Millipede

The millipede, in modest moderation,
considers *milli* an exaggeration.

NOPEDS

Matthew D. Simpson Jan. 20

The Whale

How cunning that the planet's
             largest beast, the whale,
feeds on the smallest, plankton,
             on a million scale.
Which goes to show, the mighty can't exist
unless the little ones provide the grist.

P. S. Watchers of a whale
        see mostly just a tail.

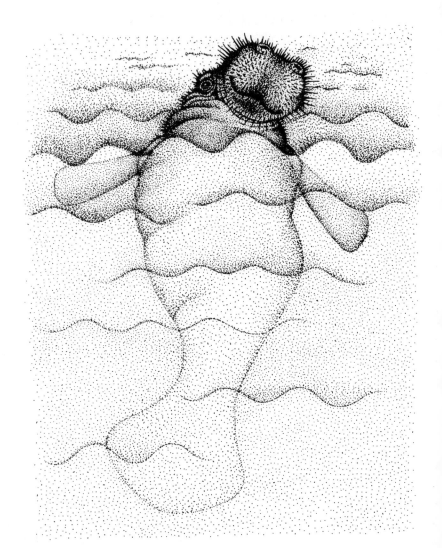

The Manatee

The ancient mariners at sea
were fancying the manatee
(which vaguely in the waves they saw)
as a fair mermaid in the raw.
Let's hope they saw, when not at sea,
maids fairer than the manatee.

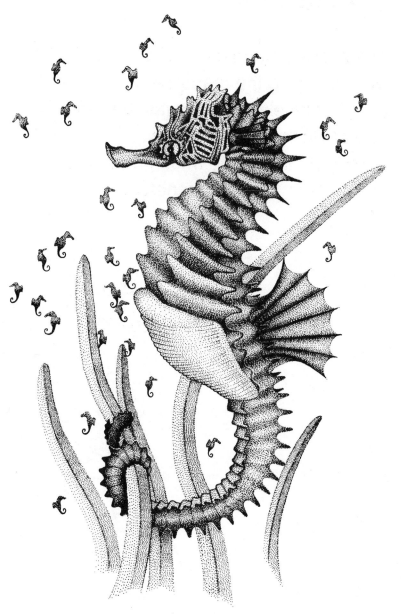

Matthew D. Simpson '91

The Sea Horse

The sea horse dad is on my list
as ultimate male chauvinist.
To give the sea colts birth and life
the sea horse doesn't trust his wife.
His lack of faith shan't be unsung:
it's he, the male, who bears the young.

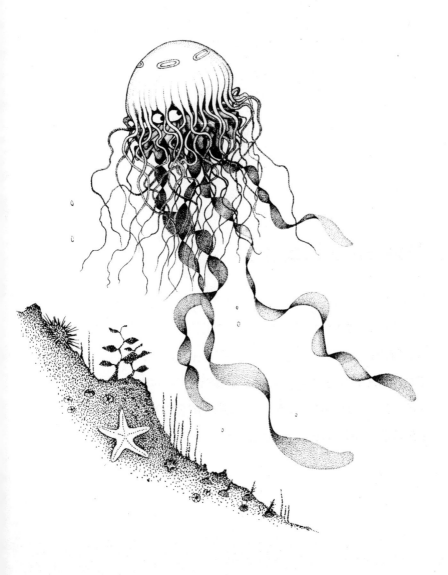

Matthew D. Simpson Feb 19, '92

The Jellyfish

The jellyfish floats in the sea,
a paragon of honesty;
for what it thinks or plans to do
is clear as glass — you see right through.
　For seafood fans, the jellyfish
is not a highly treasured dish —
the jellyfish is on the whole
less tasty than a jelly roll.
　On shore, if you're a Nervous Nelly,
you'd better not step on a jelly
for if you step on jellyfish,
it makes *you* slip and makes *it* squish.

The Starfish

The lucky starfish can survive
if he has lost one arm of five.
When it is gone, he soon won't show it
for he can readily regrow it.
  How useful this would be for man!
Especially in Pakistan
where medi-evil judges will
chop thieving hands found in the till;
or if a fool who lost his head
could grow another one instead.

The Boa

It is hard to be a predictor
of who, in a fight, will be victor.
  But there is no doubt
  who'll prevail in a bout
of a mouse and a boa constrictor.

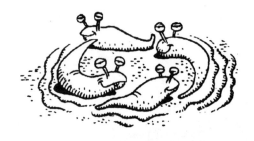

The Sea-Hare

The sea-hare mollusks
       (called Alysia Cali-Fornica)
are creatures which unusually horny are.
They are unique thanks
       to their gender status,
equipped with male and female apparatus,
and, when in love, perform as in a trance
a multimollusk ring-around-a-rosy dance.
  Oh, how convenient!
       He and she don't bother
in idle courtship-play to chase each other,
and, unlike other animals and homo,
can thus take care of everything
       pro domo.

The Oyster

Caged like a monk inside a cloister
sits in its shell the humble oyster.
Men hunt the oyster as a snack
or as an aphrodisiac,
but also to extract a pearl
to deck the bosom of a girl.
  The pearl, though,
               might prefer the oyster,
  which is less cuddly
              but more moister.

The Narwhal

The narwhal's horn is an incisor.
(You did not know this? Now you're wiser.)
He doesn't feature other teeth,
not jaw above and not beneath.
  O seniors, what sublime adventures
  to sport a horn instead of dentures!

Carp,
the Spoilsport

The nightingales extol the Lord,
the meadowlarks pass on the Word,
the pious doves assent and nod
and join them all in praising God.
The lambs are faithful Christmas props
(not knowing they will end as chops),
the praying mantis says with care
its grateful daily morning prayer . . .
They all proclaim with joy God Bless,
affirm the Word by saying Yes.
   But look, here comes a critico:
the carp complains, its mouth forms nO.
A harpist sooner will quit harping
than carps will yield
               and will quit carping.

The Earthworm

The earthworm dwells inside the earth
and sees no daylight from his birth.
He lives his life and love below,
what's up above, he doesn't know.
Methinks the worm is better off
than some of us who dwell above.

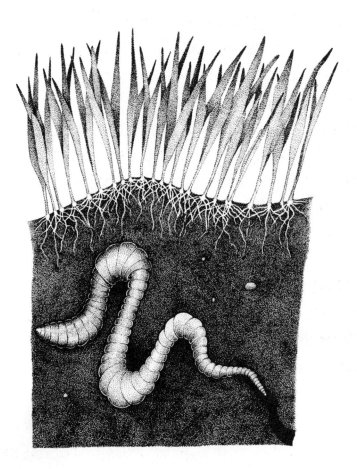

Matthew T. Simpson JAN 11, '72

MOPED?

A sullen creature is the mole.
It rarely ventures from its hole.
It throws up mounds to leave its mark
but stays down glumly in the dark.
It seems to have no joys,no hopes,
and just digs in, then sits—and mopes.

POSTSCRIPTS

Matthew D. Sampson '91 DEC 31

The Unicorn

In medieval lore was born
a horse with horn, the unicorn.
Men hunted it as best they could
and searched for it in field and wood.
For beauty horses could not match it,
and only virgin maids could catch it.
    Maybe that's why we see so few
such one-horn horses in a zoo.

The Frog Model

Of yore, on Nature's high command
a creature crawled from sea to land,
a glorious day of evolution,
a hope for many a solution.
And hopeful maidens, ever since,
have kissed a frog to find their prince.

Viruses

Viruses are a mystery.
They are not he, they are not she,
not fungi, not bacteria —
they drive me to hysteria.
They are not carp, they are not owl,
and therefore neither fish nor fowl.
They are not animal nor plant,
I want to place them but I can't.
I do not know what class to pick.
    They make me sick.

The Oonimals

I'd like to see a zany zoo
whose creatures sport the sound of oo:
like kangaroo or caribou
or cockatoo or marabou,
baboon, raccoon, or moose, or gnu.
   Can you imagine the to-do,
the fuss, ado, hullabaloo?
Folks would go wild to get a view,
they'd lose their hat,
                    they'd lose their shoe,
they would line up,
                    they'd form a queue
from Zululand and from Peru,
Kalamazoo, and Timbuctoo—
and just for what? To see the zoo
and gawk at animals with oo!

Dangerous Animal

At first in Africa it bred,
then through the world at large it spread.
It starts as egg (without a nest)
but then it feeds from mother's breast.
It is quite colorful a fellow
and comes in white, red, black,
                    and yellow.
  A few of them rise to the sky
and spread their ample wings and fly.
As predators they like to hunt
(although their teeth and claws are blunt),
and with ferociousness they kill
each other with increasing skill.
Hence while they recklessly beget,
their species is endangered yet.
  You think this beast deserves defense?
  Its name is homo sapiens.